SCIENCE STARTERS

Energy

by Rebecca Pettiford

BLASTOFF! READERS

3

BELLWETHER MEDIA • MINNEAPOLIS, MN

Note to Librarians, Teachers, and Parents:

Blastoff! Readers are carefully developed by literacy experts and combine standards-based content with developmentally appropriate text.

Level 1 provides the most support through repetition of high-frequency words, light text, predictable sentence patterns, and strong visual support.

Level 2 offers early readers a bit more challenge through varied simple sentences, increased text load, and less repetition of high-frequency words.

Level 3 advances early-fluent readers toward fluency through increased text and concept load, less reliance on visuals, longer sentences, and more literary language.

Level 4 builds reading stamina by providing more text per page, increased use of punctuation, greater variation in sentence patterns, and increasingly challenging vocabulary.

Level 5 encourages children to move from "learning to read" to "reading to learn" by providing even more text, varied writing styles, and less familiar topics.

Whichever book is right for your reader, Blastoff! Readers are the perfect books to build confidence and encourage a love of reading that will last a lifetime!

This edition first published in 2019 by Bellwether Media, Inc.

No part of this publication may be reproduced in whole or in part without written permission of the publisher. For information regarding permission, write to Bellwether Media, Inc., Attention: Permissions Department, 6012 Blue Circle Drive, Minnetonka, MN 55343.

Library of Congress Cataloging-in-Publication Data

Names: Pettiford, Rebecca, author.
Title: Energy / by Rebecca Pettiford.
Description: Minneapolis, MN : Bellwether Media, Inc., 2019. | Series: Blastoff! Readers. Science Starters
    | Includes bibliographical references and index. | Audience: 5-8. | Audience: K to 3.
Identifiers: LCCN 2017061629 (print) | LCCN 2018009249 (ebook) | ISBN 9781681035390 (ebook)
    | ISBN 9781626178069 (hardcover ; alk. paper) | ISBN 9781618914620 (pbk. ; alk. paper)
Subjects: LCSH: Force and energy–Juvenile literature. | Power resources–Juvenile literature.
Classification: LCC QC73.4 (ebook) | LCC QC73.4 .P467 2019 (print) | DDC 531/.6–dc23
LC record available at https://lccn.loc.gov/2017061629

Text copyright © 2019 by Bellwether Media, Inc. BLASTOFF! READERS and associated logos are trademarks and/or registered trademarks of Bellwether Media, Inc. SCHOLASTIC, CHILDREN'S PRESS, and associated logos are trademarks and/or registered trademarks of Scholastic Inc., 557 Broadway, New York, NY 10012.

Editor: Christina Leaf   Designer: Josh Brink

Printed in the United States of America, North Mankato, MN

Table of Contents

The car pulls into the snowy driveway. Shivering, you run into the house. You flip on the lights. Mom turns up the heat. You make hot cocoa.

Energy made all of
these things happen!

5

What Is Energy?

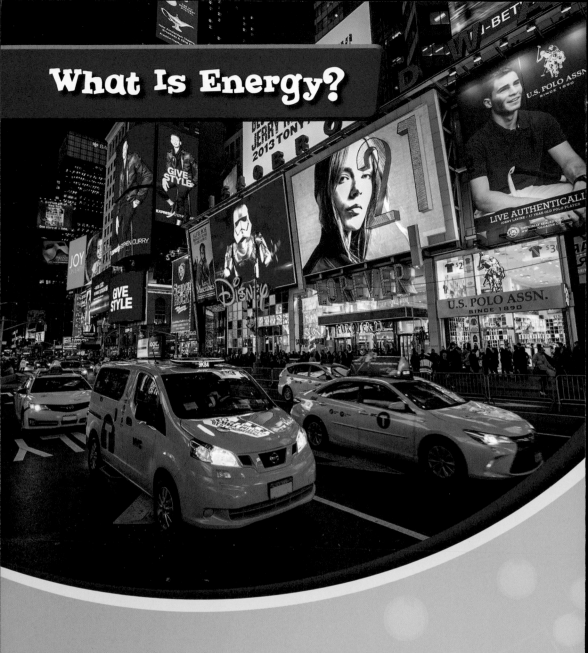

Energy makes things work.
It is everywhere!

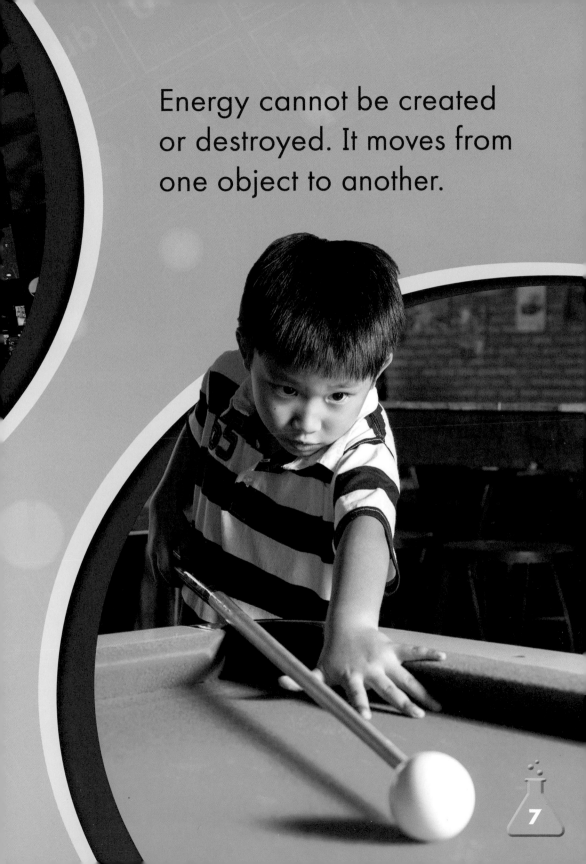

Energy cannot be created or destroyed. It moves from one object to another.

On Earth, the sun is an important **source** of energy. It gives heat and light. This makes plants grow.

People and animals eat plants. This gives them the energy they need to live.

9

Types of Energy

There are two main types of energy. **Potential energy** is stored energy. It is the energy an object has that it is not using.

potential energy

kinetic energy

When an object moves,
it has **kinetic energy**.

11

chemical
energy

Potential energy comes in different forms. **Chemical energy** is one. Objects go through a change to use this energy. Food and gasoline are examples.

An object at any height has **gravitational energy**. This potential energy is used when the object falls to the ground.

gravitational energy

Kinetic energy comes in different forms, too. Motion is an example. As an object moves faster, its kinetic energy increases.

Heat is another form.
It comes from **molecules**
or **atoms** moving quickly.

Potential energy can change to
kinetic energy. For example, the
potential energy stored in your
food changes to kinetic energy
when you eat it.

Potential and Kinetic Energy

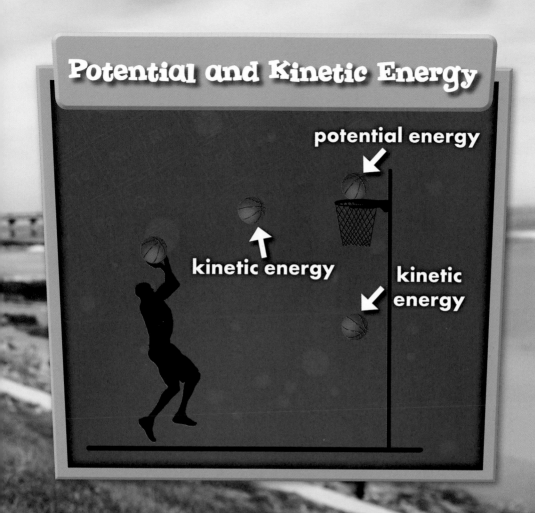

potential energy

kinetic energy

kinetic energy

You then use kinetic energy to move and think. It is the energy that keeps you alive.

Energy in Our Lives

oil refinery

Most energy comes from **nonrenewable** sources like oil and coal. There is a limited supply of these.

Renewable sources are not limited. Examples include the sun, wind, and water. **Geothermal energy** is also renewable. This is heat energy inside the Earth.

wind turbines

People use nonrenewable and renewable sources to make **electric power**. It powers lights, computers, and phones. People use it to store and cook food. Without electrical energy, life would look a lot different!

Energy Transfer

You can see how energy transfers from one ball to another!

What you will need:
- a large, heavy ball
- a smaller, lighter ball
- a large room or a place to do this activity outside

1. Hold the large ball in one hand.
2. Put the smaller ball on top of the larger ball. Hold the smaller ball still.
3. Take your hands off both balls at once. The larger ball will bounce on the ground.
4. What happens to the smaller ball? Where did that energy come from?

Glossary

atoms—units of one of the basic substances that make up the planet; atoms make up everything in the universe.

chemical energy—the potential energy that is stored in chemicals

electric power—energy that is carried through wires and powers lights and other devices

geothermal energy—heat energy within the Earth

gravitational energy—the potential energy an object has due to its position above Earth; this energy is used when gravity pulls an object downward.

kinetic energy—energy that is in motion

molecules—the smallest parts of substances that still act like the substance; molecules are made up of two or more atoms bonded together.

nonrenewable—cannot be reused

potential energy—stored energy

renewable—can be reused

source—where something starts or comes from

To Learn More

AT THE LIBRARY
Barchers, Suzanne I. *Energy*. Huntington Beach, Calif.: Teacher Created Materials, 2015.

Hawbaker, Emily. *Energy Lab for Kids: 40 Exciting Experiments to Explore, Create, Harness, and Unleash Energy*. Beverly, Mass.: Quarry, 2017.

Slade, Suzanne. *Zap!: Wile E. Coyote Experiments with Energy*. North Mankato, Minn.: Capstone Press, 2014.

ON THE WEB
Learning more about energy is as easy as 1, 2, 3.

1. Go to www.factsurfer.com.

2. Enter "energy" into the search box.

3. Click the "Surf" button and you will see a list of related web sites.

With factsurfer.com, finding more information is just a click away.

Index

The images in this book are reproduced through the courtesy of: charobnica, front cover (periodic table); John Dakapu, front cover (circuit); Sofiaworld, front cover (hero); Joseph M. Arseneau, p. 4; ulkas, p. 5; lazyllama, p. 6; Kdonmuang, p. 7; Brooke Melton, p. 8; Grigorita Ko, p. 9; Leonard Zhukovsky, pp. 10-11; Nithid Memanee, p. 12; DCrane, p. 13; FatCamera, p. 14; Mypurgatoryyears, p. 15; Daxiao Productions, pp. 16-17; Milos Kontic, p. 17 (silhouette); Graphic Box, p. 17 (basketball); Tanathip Rattaanatum, p. 18; B-L-Y, p. 19; bbernard, p. 20; Tamara JM Peterson, p. 21.